KEY TO Writing

BOOK 3

CHRISTINE MOORCROFT ◆ LES RAY

Published by Letts Educational
The Chiswick Centre
414 Chiswick High Road
London W4 5TF
Tel: 020 8996 3333
Fax: 020 8742 8390
E-mail: mail@lettsed.co.uk
Website: www.letts-education.com

Letts Educational is part of the Granada Learning Group. Granada Learning is a division of Granada plc.

First published 2003

ISBN 184085 9067

British Library Cataloguing in Publication Data
A catalogue record for this book is available from the British Library.

Concept development, design and production for Letts Educational by Start to Finish,
 9 Whitecross Square, Cheltenham GL53 7AY

Commissioned by Kate Newport
Project management by Phillipa Allum
Designed and typeset by Paul Manning
Production by PDQ
Printed and bound in Italy by Amilcare Pizzi

Introduction for Teachers or Parents

The activities in this series focus on writing skills and use a range of models.

The passages have been selected from the range of text-types advocated by the National Literacy Strategy to give the children an awareness of all types of writing, from fiction by acknowledged writers to non-fiction and real-life texts.

The passages are intended for use during shared reading activities and therefore may be more difficult than the reading age of some of the children.

The first activity in each unit encourages the children to investigate the texts and consider important features and characteristics of style. Most children should be able to complete these activities.

The second activity in each unit requires the children to use the passage as a model and to write in the style of the passage, using the important features they have identified. The writing tasks are fairly simple and short because they are related to the passage, and the skills will need to be modelled by the teacher.

The third activity in each unit fosters the development of the children's own writing. This writing is supported by photocopiable activity sheets in the Teacher's Book and so differentiation in ability level is by outcome.

An added feature of this series, from Book 3 onwards, is the inclusion of suggestions for presentation and use of ICT as an integral part of the writing process.

Contents

Nan's Story

This is a story about telling a story.

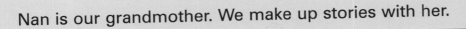

Nan is our grandmother. We make up stories with her.

This one's about a little boy who suddenly found that he couldn't get through the school door.

Why? Had he suddenly got bigger?

Someone could have helped him.

Maybe he ate something magic.

Was there a spell on him?

Perhaps an invisible force stopped him. Everyone else could go through.

Something happened to him in the night.

His name was Raymond. One night a tiny bright speck hovered above the roof of his house. It went round and round his bedroom window and then straight through the glass without a sound. Then it flitted down the road to the school. It moved in the shape of a question mark.

Perhaps he's got to answer a question before he can get through.

He might have to find something out ... find information and send it somewhere. Perhaps he has to keep finding things out and answering questions.

USEFUL WORDS

classroom, happened, home, night, past tense, peculiar, problem, school, sentence, sleep, solve, solved, spell, strange, through, title

a

1 What is Nan's story about?
2 What was Raymond's problem?
3 At first, what did the children think might have happened to him? List five things.
4 What happened during the night?

b

1 Write some ideas for a story about someone at school who has another strange problem. Make a spider diagram for recording your ideas. Here is an example:
2 Write your ideas about what caused the problem.
3 Write your ideas about how it can be solved.

> The pages were not glued.

> A strange laughing sound came from the pages.

> When other people turned the pages there was no problem.

> Other people's books closed if she tried to read them.

> **However hard she tried, her books would not open.**

> The teacher opened the books but they closed again as soon as her back was turned.

c

Use your spider diagram to help you to write a story about a strange problem for someone at school.

Write in the past tense, for example: *came* (not *come*), *closed* (not *closes*), *glued* (not *glues*), *tried* (not *tries*), *was* (not *is*).

> *Put a full stop at the end of each sentence.*

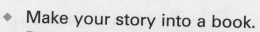

◆ Make your story into a book.
◆ Draw a picture for the cover. Write the title and your name on the cover.

MAKE YOUR WORK LOOK GOOD!

Soccer Shadows

Tom is on holiday with his family. He meets another boy on the swings. The writer tells this part of the story using dialogue.

'What's up with you, Tom?'

He turned towards the voice. Lost in his brooding, he hadn't noticed anyone else come to join him on the swings. It was a dark-haired boy of about his own age, wearing only a pair of black swimming trunks.

'Nothin',' Tom grunted. 'How d'yer know my name?'

'Heard it … on the beach … yesterday,' came back the jerky response as the boy began to work the swing higher.

'Didn't see you there.'

'I was … in the water.'

'So what's your name, then?'

'My mates … call me … Leo.'

Tom sniggered. 'What — Leo the lion?'

The boy relaxed, content now to let the swing carry him back and forth more smoothly.

'Sort of. Leo's my Zodiac sign,' he explained. 'What are you?'

Tom shrugged to show he didn't really care. 'Taurus.'

'Ah, right — the Bull.'

'Yeah, so what?'

a

1 What is the setting of the story?
2 What questions do the boys ask one another? Write three examples.
3 Write the answers they give to the questions.
4 Why do they ask one another questions?

b

1 Write two verbs which the writer uses instead of *said*.
2 Which verb shows that Tom does not feel friendly towards Leo at first?
3 Write as many verbs as you can for *said*. Copy and complete this chart:
4 What do you think happens next? Continue the dialogue.

Said quietly	Said loudly	Said angrily	Said happily
muttered	yelled	growled	chirped

c

Imagine you have just met someone of your own age on holiday.

◆ Write some of the things you might say to him or her.
◆ Write the answers which he or she might give.
◆ Write the questions and answers as a dialogue, using speech marks.

◆ Re-draft the dialogue, starting a new line for each new speaker.
◆ Draw a scene from the dialogue. Use speech bubbles to show what the characters say.

MAKE YOUR WORK LOOK GOOD!

No Problem, Davy

Davy is on holiday in Corfu. He goes for a ride in a horse-drawn carriage.

They drove past colourful gardens and open-air cafés with bright yellow chairs arranged in the cool shade of the trees. They drove down a long hill alongside the bluest sea Davy had ever seen. They drove along a wide avenue of tall houses and shops, then along a busy street full of cars and bikes and people on holiday

wearing shorts and sun hats. Here and there were stalls and barrows piled high with apples, peaches, melons, bananas, oranges and lemons. Davy thought he'd like to buy a peach.

Lots of little side-streets branched away uphill. At the bottom of one of the streets a car was moving to and fro, trying to turn around in the narrow space. On the street corner stood one of the barrows of delicious fruit.

USEFUL WORDS

along, alongside, around, behind, delicious, description, down, drive, drove, here, in, in front of, inside, move, moved, near, next to, past, stood, there, verb, walk, walked

a

1. The description of the setting is colourful. Which two colours are named?
2. Are the colours bright or dull? Give an example.
3. Davy can see other colours which are not named. What colours are these?
4. What is the weather like? How can you tell?

b

1. List the words in the passage which show where things were or where they moved to or from, for example: *along*, *by*.
2. List the verbs which show that Davy and other people and things were moving.
3. Continue the description of the setting. Write it as if Davy were moving through it. The picture will help.

c

Think about a place you have visited.

- List the things you noticed. Write what colours they were.
- Write some words which say where things were.
- Write some verbs to show how you moved and how other things moved.
- Write a description of how you moved through the place.

- Draw a picture of the place you have visited.
- Use different coloured pens to write sentences from your description on separate pieces of paper. Glue the sentences around the picture.

MAKE YOUR WORK LOOK GOOD!

Story Openings and Endings

Openings and endings like these can be found in many different books.

A Once upon a time in London,

B There was once a boy named Jack.

C Long ago two sisters lived in a small cottage.

D One Saturday afternoon Jenna was watching television.

E Many years ago in Cardiff

F It was in the middle of winter and the garden was white with frost.

G He remembered that day for the rest of his life.

H He never did it again.

I That is why there are no snakes in Ireland.

J That is how we know about the old Roman town.

K Now, every time she sees a feather, she remembers that night.

L From that day on she never ate chicken.

USEFUL WORDS after, after that, character, ending, from that day on, it was, long ago, many years ago, once, once upon a time, one day, opening, that is why, there was once

a

1 What do the openings tell you about the stories? Record your answers on a chart.

Opening	Place	Time	Characters
A			
B			

2 What do the endings tell you about the stories? Record your answers on a chart.

Ending	What it says about the story
G	
H	

b

1 Read the openings of three other stories. What do they tell you about the stories? Copy and complete the chart.

Story title	Opening sentence	What it says about the story		
		Place	Time	Characters

2 a) Copy the endings of the stories. In the books, cover the endings of each story. Ask a friend to match the endings to the stories.

b) How did you know which ending matched which story?

c

Re-read a story which you have written.

- Copy the opening sentence of your story. Does it tell the reader about the place, the time and the people?
- Change the opening, using what you have learned.
- Re-write the ending, using what you have learned.

Write the opening and ending of your story using a computer. Use an interesting and colourful font.

MAKE YOUR WORK LOOK GOOD!

5 The Hundred-Mile-an-Hour Dog

This story has been split into chapters. Each chapter is split into paragraphs. A paragraph can have one sentence or many. The writer begins a new paragraph when he starts writing about a new idea.

Streaker is a mixed-up kind of dog. You can see from her thin body and powerful legs that she's got a lot of greyhound blood in her, along with quite a bit of Ferrari and a large chunk of whirlwind.

Nobody in our family likes walking her and this is hardly surprising. Streaker can out-accelerate a torpedo. She can do 0 to 100 mph in the blink of an eye. She's usually vanished over the far horizon long before you have time to yell — 'Streaker!'

Dad refuses to walk her, point-blank. 'I've got backache,' is his usual excuse, though how this stops him from walking I really haven't a clue.

I tried something similar once myself. 'I've got front-ache,' I said. Mum gave me a chilly glare and handed me the dog-lead. She'll do anything to get out of walking Streaker, too, and that is how the whole thing started. I ended up having the craziest Easter holiday you can imagine.

'Trevor …' said Mum one morning at the beginning of the holiday, and she gave me one of her really big, innocent smiles.

USEFUL WORDS

anything, before, begin, chapter, character, excuse, hardly, idea, indent, information, introduce, myself, new, paragraph, powerful, sentence, similar, start, surprising, torpedo, though, usually, vanished

1 How many paragraphs are there in the passage?

2 How can you tell when a new paragraph starts?

3 What does the first paragraph tell you about Streaker?

a

To answer these questions, write the first six words of the paragraph.

1 Which paragraph says why no one wants to walk Streaker?

2 Which paragraph says that Trevor's mum is going to ask him to do something?

3 Which paragraph says that Trevor doesn't like walking Streaker?

4 Which paragraph introduces Streaker?

5 Which paragraph says that Trevor's dad never walks Streaker?

b

Write five paragraphs for a story about a pet.

♦ The first paragraph should introduce the pet.

♦ In the other paragraphs you could say more about the pet and introduce other characters to your story.

You could give the reader an idea of what might happen in the story.

c

♦ Word-process your story.

♦ Add a picture box and put a picture of the pet in it.

MAKE YOUR WORK LOOK GOOD!

The Story of Persephone

Zeus, the king of the gods, and Demeter, the goddess of grain, had a daughter named Persephone.

One day Persephone was picking flowers. She reached out to pick the most beautiful of them all — a narcissus. As she touched the flower the earth opened and Hades, the king of the Underworld, rushed out in his golden chariot, seized her and took her home to be his wife.

Demeter searched and searched for Persephone. She neither ate nor drank for nine days. Then on the tenth day the Sun god Helios told Demeter what had happened. He said that Zeus had planned it with Hades.

Demeter was furious. She went down from Mount Olympus, the home of the gods, into the land of mortals. She would not let the crops grow until Persephone came back. So no seed sprouted. No barley, wheat or oats or any other grain grew in the fields.

Eventually Zeus sent his messenger Hermes to the Underworld. Hermes told Hades what was happening on the earth and asked if Persephone could go back to her mother. Hades agreed that Persephone could spend most of each year with her mother but for part of the year she must stay with him.

And that is how the seasons came about.

USEFUL WORDS

as, beautiful, character, eventually, first, furious, neither, next, nor, one day, pact, power, punishment, revenge, so, theme, then, would

1 What is the first thing which happens in the story?
Write your answer in note form.

2 What happens next? Write in note form.

3 List the main events of the story in order.
Write in note form. You could write
on a flow chart like this:

When you write in note form, you leave out the less important words.

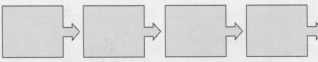

Main events of the story of Persephone

a

The themes of the story of Persephone are power, punishment and making pacts.

1 Which characters show their power, and how?

2 Who is punished? Who does the punishing, and how?

3 What pact is made?

b

Read another story about Greek gods and goddesses.

♦ Write the main events of the story.

♦ Using your notes only, re-tell the story.

c

♦ Use a computer to print some letters of the Greek alphabet.

♦ Print the letters in different colours and sizes. Use them to decorate your story.

MAKE YOUR WORK LOOK GOOD!

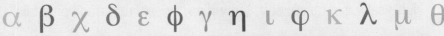

Goldilocks

A story map is one way of putting the events of a story in order. You can follow the story of Goldilocks, a traditional tale for younger children, on this story map.

woods

a little house

porridge

just right

too salty

too sweet

Goldilocks

kitchen

too hard

living room

just right

too soft

three bears

bedroom

just right

too low

too high

USEFUL WORDS

big, character, hard, high, just, little, low, medium-sized, middle-sized, right, salty, sentence, soft, story map, sweet, too, traditional tale

a

1 Who is the main character of the story?
2 Where does the story begin?
3 What does Goldilocks find there?
4 List the three rooms into which Goldilocks goes.

b

Use the story map to help you re-tell the story for a child of about five.

1 Write what Goldilocks does in each room of the house.
2 What happens at the end of the story?
3 What might each bear say?

> *Use simple words. Write short sentences.*

c

Use a story map to help you re-tell the story of *Puss in Boots*.

- Draw the places.
- Draw what happens there.
- Write headings.
- Write the story.

Make a concertina book and write your story in it. You could use one page for writing and the next for a picture.

MAKE YOUR WORK LOOK GOOD!

The Legend of Rama and Sita

This is a Hindu legend which is celebrated at the festival of Divali.

The nurse said to Queen Kaykai, 'Your son Bharata should be the next king of Ayodhya. You saved the king's life and he promised you two wishes. Make him name Bharata his heir and send Rama away.'

So the queen reminded the king of his promise. He turned pale. He pleaded with Kaykai: 'The people love Rama.' Kaykai would not listen, so the king sent Rama and his wife Sita away to live in the forest.

Demons lived in the forest. Their king was a ten-headed monster named Ravana. One day while Rama was hunting, Ravana sent a fawn with a broken leg to Sita. As she went to help it he pounced on her and carried her off to his palace on the island of Lanka.

Rama's brave brother, Lakshmana, came to help him to find Sita. Hanuman the monkey king called all the monkeys of India to help. They searched and searched until they found Sita.

Some of the monkeys made themselves into a great bridge across the sea to Lanka. Others ran across it and fired their bows at Ravana.

Finally Rama had one magic arrow left. He aimed it at Ravana's heart. The ten heads screamed and Ravana fell to the ground.

Rama and Sita led their great army of monkeys back to Ayodhya. The people hung lamps in their windows to welcome them back.

USEFUL WORDS

carried, celebrated, character, evil, festival, fight, fired, good, legend, lose, people, pleaded, plot, pounced, searched, struggle, themselves

a

1 List the characters in the story.
2 Which characters are good? How can you tell?
3 Which characters are evil? How can you tell?
   You could write your
   answers on a chart
   like this:

Good characters	How I can tell	Evil characters	How I can tell

b

1 Which character in the story would you choose as a friend?
2 List the reasons you would choose him or her.
3 Choose some words from the word bank which describe the character.

Word bank

brave   honest
clever   kind
dependable   loyal
gentle   strong
helpful   truthful

c

Imagine you are one of the monkeys in the story (who can speak and write). Write a letter to another monkey who was not there, telling him or her about Ravana.

◆ Use a computer to design a letterhead.
◆ Remember to make up an address and date.

MAKE YOUR WORK LOOK GOOD!

The Parable of the Seeds

A parable is a story which explains something. In the Christian Bible, Jesus used parables to teach people.

Jesus said, 'A farmer went out to sow some seeds. Some seeds fell on the edge of the path. Birds ate them. Some seeds fell on to stones and rocks where there was little soil. They sprang up but as soon as the sun shone they withered. Their roots were weak and they died. Some fell among thorns and weeds and were choked. Others fell on to rich soil. They grew strong and healthy and gave a rich harvest.'

Then Jesus explained the story. He said that the seeds were the words of God. Those on the path were heard by people but they did not take root in people's hearts. They were soon lost. Those on the rocks were welcomed by people, but if those people faced anything difficult they quickly forgot about the words of God.

Jesus said that those which fell among the thorns and weeds were heard by people but ignored because those people were more interested in material things and money.

The seeds which fell on to rich soil were the words of God which people heard and understood and remembered. People shared this harvest with others.

USEFUL WORDS

audience, Bible, character, choked, explained, explanation, grew, harvest, healthy, heard, Jesus, meaning, outcome, parable, people, remembered, seeds, setting, sow, sprang, strong, understood, weak

a

1 In this parable, what was Jesus explaining to people?
2 In a parable one thing is used to stand for something else. What did the seeds stand for in this parable?
3 Copy and complete this chart about the parable of the seeds.

Where the seeds landed	What happened to them	What happened to the words of God
on the edge of the path		
on stones and rocks		
among thorns and weeds		
on rich soil		

b

1 Jesus told this parable to people who farmed. They knew about sowing seeds. What is the setting of the parable?
2 If Jesus told the parable today, what setting might he use for:
   a) children?   **b)** sportspeople?   **c)** cooks?
3 Describe a new setting and audience for this parable today.

c

Plan your own modern version of the parable. Make notes about:

- the setting
- what happens
- what will stand for the words of God
- the people who will hear the parable
- bad outcomes and a good outcome
- what the parable means.

Write your parable in your neatest handwriting. Start each paragraph with a decorated letter.

MAKE YOUR WORK LOOK GOOD!

The Little Match Girl

This is an old story with a sad ending.

It was New Year's Eve. It was snowing and darkness was falling. A little girl with bare feet trudged along the street carrying bundles of matches. No one bought any, so she had no money to take home.

She sheltered between two houses. She could see a fire burning in a hearth and people sitting around a table. She shivered and struck a match. She felt a little warmer. She imagined she was sitting in front of a warm stove. Then the flame went out.

She huddled into the corner and struck another match. She saw a roast goose on the table. The goose stepped off the table and waddled across the floor.

She struck another match. She saw a Christmas tree, with candles on it. As the match went out, the candles seemed to rise into the sky and become stars. But one of them fell and made a long streak in the sky.

'Ah! Someone is dying,' she said, for her grandmother had told her that when a star falls from the sky someone dies.

She struck another match. She saw her grandmother. She called, 'Take me with you, Grandma! You'll be gone when the match goes out, just like the stove and the goose and the Christmas tree.'

New Year's Day dawned. Between two houses lay a little girl with rosy cheeks and a smile on her face — frozen to death on the last night of the year. She was no longer sad. Perhaps she was with her grandmother.

USEFUL WORDS

another, become, bought, darkness, ending, flame, grandmother, huddled, imagined, outdoors, setting, snowing, someone, trudged

1 Describe the setting of the story.
You could use headings:
Time, *Place* and *Weather*.

2 Who is the main character?

3 Why is she outdoors on a cold night?

4 How do you feel about her?

a

1 List the things which make the story sad.

2 Think of ways of changing the story to give it a happy ending.
Write your ideas on
a chart like this:

Changing the setting	Adding new characters	Adding new events

b

Re-write the story so that it has a
happy ending. Introduce a new
character who can change the ending
of the story.

Use your notes from b to help you.

c

◆ Use a computer to print some paper with a
background of snowflakes and stars.

◆ Hand-write or word-process your story on this paper.

MAKE YOUR WORK
LOOK GOOD!

The Spell Which Went Wrong

Mr Majeika is a teacher who casts spells, but they often go wrong.

Everything went black, and there were flashing lights and very odd noises. Class Three felt as if they were being whirled round and round. Then the noises died down, and it started to get light again.

'Phew! That's a relief,' said Mr Majeika. 'I really didn't think the spell would work. But look, the computer has vanished.'

'Wait a minute, Mr Majeika,' said Jody. 'We can't see the computer, but where do you think we are?'

'In our classroom as usual,' said Thomas. 'Look, there are the tables and chairs.'

'But there's something funny going on,' said Pete. 'There's a huge window of glass between us and the rest of the room.'

'Yes,' said Jody, 'and if you turn round, what's behind us?' Thomas and Pete turned.

'The whole wall is glowing!' said Thomas.

'And there are giant words on it,' said Pete.

'Yes,' said Mr Majeika. 'It says, "Ha! ha! You've really gone and done it now, you silly idiot".'

'I'm awfully afraid, Mr Majeika,' said Jody, 'that your spell has made things far worse. Don't you realise where we are? We're inside the computer — between the glass and the screen! And I don't know how we'll ever get out.'

USEFUL WORDS

after, afterwards, beginning, end, episode, event, happen, happened, huge, middle, next, problem, sequel, sequence, solve, something, usual, whole

1 From where in the story do you think this passage is taken — the beginning, the middle or the end?

2 What is the setting for the story?

3 Who is the main character?

4 Who are the other characters?

a

1 What is the problem faced by Mr Majeika and his class?

2 What do you think caused the problem?

3 What can Mr Majeika and the children do to solve their problem? Discuss this with your group and write your ideas.

b

Write the next part of the story.

♦ Describe how Mr Majeika and the children solve their problem.

♦ At the end of the story introduce a new problem.

c

♦ Type the passage on a computer.

♦ In a separate document, type your ending to the story. Others can do the same.

♦ Collect the different endings together so that readers can choose their own ending.

MAKE YOUR WORK LOOK GOOD!

George's Ghastly Grandma

This story begins by describing George's grandma.

George sat himself down at the table in the kitchen. He was shaking a little. Oh, how he hated Grandma! He really hated that horrid old witchy woman. And all of a sudden he had a tremendous urge to do something about her. Something whopping. Something absolutely terrific. A real shocker. A sort of explosion. He wanted to blow away the witchy smell that hung about her in the next room. He may have been only eight years old but he was a brave little boy. He was ready to take this old woman on.

'I'm not going to be frightened by her,' he said softly to himself. But he was frightened. And that's why he wanted suddenly to explode her away.

Well … not quite away. But he wanted to shake her up a bit.

Very well, then. What should it be, this whopping terrific exploding shocker for Grandma?

He would have liked to put a firework banger under her chair but he didn't have one.

He would have liked to put a long green snake down the back of her dress but he didn't have a long green snake. He would have liked to put six big black rats in the room with her and lock the door but he didn't have six big black rats.

As George sat there pondering this interesting problem his eye fell upon the bottle of Grandma's brown medicine.

USEFUL WORDS

first, he, her, him, himself, horrid, I, it, me, my, noun, person, pronoun, she, suddenly, they, third, tremendous, us, verb, we, woman, you

1 What is George's problem?
2 List some of the things he wants
to do to solve his problem.
3 What do you think he will do?
4 What makes you think this?

a

---

1 List the pronouns which the writer uses instead
of repeating the nouns *George* and *Grandma*.
Copy and
complete
this chart:

Pronouns for *George*	Pronouns for *George's*	Pronouns for *Grandma*	Pronouns for *Grandma's*

2 If the story were written as if George were telling it, which
pronouns would be used instead of *George*?

b

Re-write the passage as if you were George, telling your own
story.

◆ Think about the pronouns you will use.
◆ Check that the verbs agree with the pronouns, for example:
he was and *I was* are both correct.

c

◆ Use a computer to word-process the passage and
change the pronouns.
◆ Add some pictures of George with thought bubbles
showing what he would like to do.

MAKE YOUR WORK
LOOK GOOD!

Charlotte's Web

Charlotte's Web is a long story. It is split into twenty-two chapters; each chapter has a title. These summaries tell you what some of the chapters are about.

CHAPTER 1 Before breakfast

This introduces the Arable family and the main character Fern Arable and their farm. Mr Arable plans to kill a new-born piglet because he thinks it is too weak to survive, but Fern pleads with him to let her look after it. She looks after the piglet and names him Wilbur.

CHAPTER 2 Wilbur

Fern and her family look after Wilbur. He grows up and Mr Arable wants to sell him. Fern pleads with him to let Wilbur stay. They agree that he can go to her Uncle Homer's farm; he sometimes keeps a pig until it is much bigger.

CHAPTER 3 Escape

Wilbur lives in the barn at Uncle Homer's farm and Fern visits him nearly every day. Wilbur is bored, so a goose tells him how he can get out into the orchard. He escapes! However he is soon caught and sent back to the barn.

CHAPTER 4 Loneliness

Wilbur looks for someone to play with. The lamb will not talk to him. Templeton the rat will not play with him. Wilbur is lonely because he has no friends. He goes out into the yard, lies down and sobs. Uncle Homer thinks he is ill and sends his son to give him some medicine. Then, after dark, a little voice says, 'I'll be your friend. I've watched you all day and I like you.'

USEFUL WORDS

because, bigger, caught, chapter, character, friend, heading, however, lamb, medicine, number, plead, setting, someone, sometimes, spider diagram, summary, survive

1 What do the chapter titles and summaries tell you about the setting of the story?
2 Name the characters and write what you know about them.
3 How do you feel towards Wilbur?
4 Whose do you think is the little voice which Wilbur hears?

a

1 Write the title of another long story you know.
2 Write the chapter titles.
3 Write summaries of the first four chapters. List the main events.

b

Plan a long story of your own.

◆ Use a spider diagram to collect ideas (see page 5).
◆ Write the titles of the chapters.
◆ Under each title write notes on what the chapter will be about.

c

◆ Design a title page for each chapter.
◆ Word-process your story. Choose different fonts for the chapter titles and for the rest of the text.

MAKE YOUR WORK LOOK GOOD!

Cooking in Jórvík

This is from an information book about Jórvík, the old Norse settlement in York.

The Norse people (sometimes called Vikings) settled in Jórvík in the tenth century.

Most houses had a fire in the centre of the main room. Cooking pots hung from a wooden or iron frame over the fire. Rich people might have an iron spit on which meat was roasted.

Archaeologists have found clay and iron pots and pans. They even found an iron frying pan with a wooden handle. Baskets, buckets and pottery jars were used for storing foods, and most homes would have a kettle made of iron or clay in which a meal was cooked. Traces of stew have been found on pieces from these kettles.

Many burnt fist-sized stones have been found in the fireplaces. These stones were heated in the fire and then placed in pots of water or soup to boil it. They were re-heated and re-used until they broke up.

Spoons and ladles made of wood and bone, and iron knives of different sizes, have been found. The only forks found were large ones used in cooking. People ate with their fingers.

 USEFUL WORDS
archaeologists, centre, century, chart, facts, heading, information, iron, metal, non-fiction, pottery, settlement, source, summary, wooden

1 What is the passage about?
2 How do we know about this settlement?
3 Which of the following information can you find out from the passage: clothes, cooking, food, heating, homes, money, religion, trade, warfare?

a

1 Use a chart like this to record information from the passage:

What the homes were like	How people cooked	What people ate	How they kept warm

Write in note form.

2 Find out more about homes in Norse settlements in Britain from information books. Make notes on your chart.
3 Using your notes only, write about how people cooked and what they ate in Jórvík.

b

Find information about something else in history.

◆ Before you begin, plan a chart for recording what you find out.
◆ Use more than one source of information.
◆ Make notes on your chart.

c

◆ Use different coloured pens to record information from different sources.
◆ Make a key to show which sources you used.

MAKE YOUR WORK
LOOK GOOD!

15 Insects

This is a non-chronological report about insects.

There are thousands of different kinds of insects. There are more kinds of insects than there are mammals, fish, birds and reptiles put together. There are some ways in which all insects are similar.

butterfly

bee

ladybird

ant

These are all insects.

All adult insects have three parts to their bodies: a head, a thorax (the middle part) and an abdomen (the lower part). On their heads they have antennae (feelers). They use these for smelling and feeling. Most adult insects have a pair of large eyes.

They have three pairs of legs attached to the thorax. Most adult insects have wings attached to the thorax. Some have one pair of wings; others have two pairs. Some ants and aphids have no wings.

Insects lay eggs. After an egg hatches the young insect is called a larva or a maggot. A caterpillar is the larva of a moth or butterfly. Some young insects change their shapes several times before they become adults.

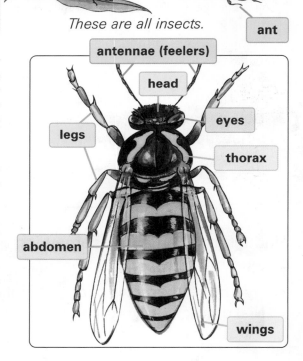

antennae (feelers)

head

eyes

legs

thorax

abdomen

wings

USEFUL WORDS

abdomen, adult, caption, caterpillar, chart, diagram, feelers, hatch, information, insect, label, larva, mammal, non-chronological, report, reptile, sentence, similar, thorax, verb

1 How is the passage different from a story about an insect?

2 What facts does the passage give? Copy and complete the chart.

Insect facts			
Facts about bodies	Facts about heads	Facts about legs and wings	Facts about young insects

a

---

1 Copy and complete this chart about the animals listed:

Animal	Does its body have three parts?	Does it have three pairs of legs?	Does it have feelers?
beetle			
snail			
spider			
woodlouse			

b

2 Read the insect facts chart you made in **a**.
Which animal is an insect? Which are not insects?

Find out about spiders. Use information texts.

◆ On a chart, record information about their bodies, head and legs and about their young.

◆ Write a non-chronological report about spiders.

c

◆ Draw and label pictures of different kinds of spiders.

◆ Combine your pictures and report to make an information leaflet about spiders.

MAKE YOUR WORK
LOOK GOOD!

Spoon Bells

These instructions tell you how to make the sound of bells using spoons.

You need:
- a piece of string 1 metre long
- 2 spoons

DO THIS:

1 Tie a spoon to the middle of the string like this:

2 Hold the ends of the string like this:

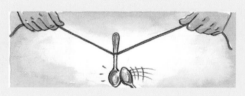

Ask a friend to tap the spoon with the other spoon. You should hear a tapping sound.

3 Hold the ends of the string to your ears, like this:

Ask a friend to tap the spoon with the other spoon. You should hear a sound like bells ringing.

This is because sound travels better along a solid material (like string) than it does through air.

USEFUL WORDS
arrow, bullet point, friend, instruction, materials, metre, number, order, piece, ringing, sequence, sound, spoon, string, tapping, tell, through, travels, verb

1 What do the instructions help you to do?
2 How do you know what you will need?
3 How do you know in which order to do things?
4 What helps you to follow the instructions?
5 How do you know if you have followed them properly?

a

1 List the verbs from the instructions.
2 What do you notice about the verbs?
3 Use the instructions to help you to make spoon bells.

b

Make notes about something you have made.

- List the materials you used.
- Write what you did.
- Re-write this as instructions.

c

- Draw pictures or diagrams to make your instructions easy to understand.
- Number each step of the instructions. You could use arrows or bullet points.

MAKE YOUR WORK
LOOK GOOD!

35

Too Much Television?

These people have different reasons for their opinions.

> We can learn a lot from television programmes.

Rhys, aged 10

> It is better for children to be outdoors in the fresh air than indoors watching television.

Nina, aged 32, mother of seven

> Watching television is a good way of learning new words, like 'arbitration'.

Dr Leeva Malone, aged 52, psychologist

> Television is taking the place of books. I say it should be banned.

Major Whippam, aged 126, retired SAS fighter

> If I never watched television I would never know what it was really like in far off countries

Mary, aged 8

> Watching TV makes children fat and lazy. They should be running around, not slumped in a chair.

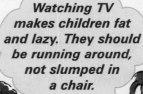

James Fitt, aged 49

USEFUL WORDS

against, arbitration, banned, because, countries, if, for, opinion, programme, really, reason, right, running, should, should not, slumped, taking, television, think, view, why, wrong

1 Who think that television is *not* bad for children?
2 Who think television *is* bad for children?
3 What reasons are given for and against children watching television? Copy and complete the chart.

Children watching television	
Reasons for	**Reasons against**

4 Write a summary of both sides of the argument.

a

1 Make a chart similar to the one above.
2 On it write notes about the following argument:

We heard people complaining because chips were no longer to be served for school dinners. Some children said it wasn't fair because they should be encouraged to make their own choices instead of having choices made for them. Others said it was a good idea because chips make you fat.

"They only make you fat if you eat millions of them every day," said one boy. He added that they could be served once a week. His friend said that it would make our diet worse not better because if you are forbidden something you only want it more.

b

Collect opinions about taking chips off the menu at school.

◆ Collect the opinions on a chart.
◆ Write a summary of the argument.

c

Draw pictures of the argument with speech bubbles.

> MAKE YOUR WORK LOOK GOOD!

Message Board

This is the message board in Sara's kitchen.

A Jack — lunch in fridge. Enjoy! Love Joy xxx

B Pay paper bill 4 weeks

C Mum
Can't find Kipper.
Haven't seen him all day.
Opened a tin of 'Posh Kat' for him.
Hasn't eaten it.
Worried.
Love Sammy
xxxx

D Sunday
Nan's birthday
60

E 10 July 7 p.m.
Meeting about new road
Community Centre

F Mum
No swimming club today.
Sara. xxx

G Bill 01236 557800
Ann 09861 668905

H To all
Please switch dishwasher on when full.
It's not magic.
Signed Mum

I cat food   cotton
milk   wool
apples   pasta
bread   butter
washing-   pizza
  up liquid

USEFUL WORDS

brief, dishwasher, magic, message, note, pizza, please, punctuation, quick, sentence, short, signed, swimming, switch, washing-up liquid, worried

Copy and complete the chart to answer questions 1 and 2.

1 Which notes are written for another person to read? How can you tell?

2 Which notes are written only for the writer to read? How can you tell?

Note	Is it for another person to read?	How I can tell
A		

a

1 Re-write notes A, C, F and H as letters.
- ◆ Begin with a greeting and sign off the letters.
- ◆ Write complete sentences.

How do these changes affect the 'feel' of the notes?

2 Re-write notes B, D, E, G and I in complete sentences. How do these changes affect the 'feel' of the notes?

3 Explain why people do not write notes like these in sentences.

b

Write notes for these people to put on their message boards:

I must remember Mothers' Day on Sunday. I need to buy a present for Mum. I think I'll buy flowers. I need to buy a card for her, too.

I have to take my reading book to school. I need my football kit. I mustn't forget my lunchbox or homework.

c

Write your notes on pieces of paper with interesting shapes. Draw colourful borders for them.

MAKE YOUR WORK LOOK GOOD!

Two Letters

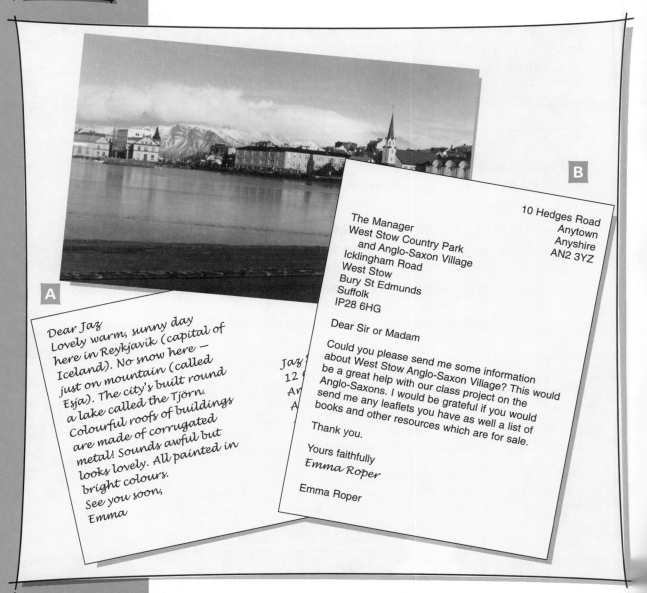

A

Dear Jaz
Lovely warm, sunny day
here in Reykjavik (capital of
Iceland). No snow here —
just on mountain (called
Esja). The city's built round
a lake called the Tjörn.
Colourful roofs of buildings
are made of corrugated
metal! Sounds awful but
looks lovely. All painted in
bright colours.
See you soon,
Emma

B

10 Hedges Road
Anytown
Anyshire
AN2 3YZ

The Manager
West Stow Country Park
   and Anglo-Saxon Village
Icklingham Road
West Stow
Bury St Edmunds
Suffolk
IP28 6HG

Dear Sir or Madam

Could you please send me some information
about West Stow Anglo-Saxon Village? This would
be a great help with our class project on the
Anglo-Saxons. I would be grateful if you would
send me any leaflets you have as well a list of
books and other resources which are for sale.

Thank you.

Yours faithfully
Emma Roper

Emma Roper

Jaz
12
A

USEFUL WORDS

avenue, awful, buildings, built, colourful, dear, faithfully, from,
information, lane, love, lovely, madam, mountain, postcard, postcode,
purpose, resources, road, sign, sincerely, sir, street, sunny, yours

1 What is the purpose of each piece of writing?
2 Where would you find each type of writing?
3 To whom could the writer send each one? Copy and complete this chart:

Text	To someone the writer knows well or to a stranger	How I can tell
A		
B		

a

1 How does the writer begin the postcard **A**?
2 How does she begin the letter **B**?
3 Why does she begin them differently?
4 How does she sign off each message? Explain why she signs them off differently.

b

Re-write the postcard as a letter to someone you do not know well who has asked for information about Reykjavík.

◆ Write the information which is on the postcard.
◆ Change the way in which you write it.
◆ Underline the parts you have changed.

c

◆ Word-process your letter, putting your own address at the top.
◆ Write the address on an envelope in the correct style.

MAKE YOUR WORK LOOK GOOD!

AUTUMN AD51

THE CELTIC TIMES

ALL THE NEWS
AT LEAST TWICE PER YEAR

CARATACUS TAKEN BY ROMANS

Brave defence by Caratacus

By our battle correspondent, Regidubnus

Caratacus of the Catuvellauni was the best hope British tribes had of resisting the invading Romans until Cartimandua, the queen of the Brigantes, turned traitor and handed him over to the Romans. But he made a clever escape and began to build up his forces again — this time in Wales.

So great was the renown of Caratacus that the Roman Emperor Claudius himself came to Britain to lead his troops into battle. He met Caratacus and his brave band of fighters at the River Medway in Kent. Caratacus and his men held out for two days, but in the end they

were no match for Claudius and his forty thousand soldiers.

"The river ran red with the blood of the brave Catuvellauni and Welshmen," said Cogidubnus, 31, a follower of Caratacus.

Claudius has taken Caratacus as a prisoner to Rome. Eleven British tribes have now surrendered to the Romans and Britain has a Roman governor, Aulus Plautius.

USEFUL WORDS

after, and, article, battle, correspondent, first, if, governor, headline, meanwhile, newspaper, recount, renown, since, soldier, spoken, subheading, that, then, when, which, while, who

Latest news — Caratacus taken by Romans!

a

1 What does the headline tell you that the news article is about?
2 What are the main events of the report?
3 Write a subheading for each of these events.
4 As well as recounting the events, the report gives information. List the main points.

b

1 Which words in the passage tell you about the order of the events?
2 Write three other words which can be used to show the order of events.
3 Which words in the passage were spoken? How can you tell?
4 Write the story of the Roman invasion as a letter from a Roman soldier to his family at home. Use the notes you made in **a**.

c

Re-read a recount you have written about an event in history.
Re-write it as a newspaper article.

♦ Write and edit your newspaper article using a computer.
♦ Use desktop publishing software to make it look like a real newspaper article.

MAKE YOUR WORK LOOK GOOD!

Make It Snappy

A

SPENDING too much time sitting watching television or playing computer games is making the nation's children unfit and overweight. In addition to this most of them are taken to school by car, and so have no opportunity to walk. This lack of exercise, plus the growing trend of eating 'junk' foods such as sweets, crisps and fizzy drinks, is not helping.

'Parents can help children to stay fit by making the effort to walk to school or at least to walk part of the journey if it is too long,' says Dr Jogg of Hothouse University.

B

LAURA SPRITE believes in fairies. She can prove they exist. She is about to publish a book of photographs of fairies at the bottom of her garden. 'Many people do not believe that fairies exist,' says Laura, 'because they do not look for them properly and, when they do, they cannot see them.' She has developed almost a sixth sense and can always spot them.

Laura points out that another reason why people do not believe in fairies is because they do not normally show up on photographs but, by developing special techniques (which are a closely-guarded secret), she has been able to make them show up on film.

USEFUL WORDS

according to, another, believes, brief, closely, developed, guarded, headline, journey, main, paragraph, point, special, subheading, summarise, summary, techniques, television

1 Copy and complete the chart
to answer the following questions:

Passage	Subject	Main points
A		
B		

   a) What is the subject of each
passage?

   b) What are the main points
of each passage?

2 Write a headline for each passage. The headline must tell the
reader the subject.

3 Write subheadings for each passage. The subheadings must tell
the reader the main points.

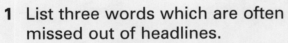

1 List three words which are often
missed out of headlines.

2 Why are these words missed out?

3 Write a sentence to summarise each
passage.

A sentence must make sense. It must contain a verb.

Make notes about something in the news which interests you.

- Write the main points.
- Write a headline and subheadings.
- Write a paragraph under each subheading.

- Use a computer to make your writing look like a real
newspaper article.
- Draw a picture to illustrate it.

MAKE YOUR WORK
LOOK GOOD!

A Treasure Chest of Words

As lonely as a cloud

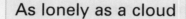

A smudge of a girl

Necks like rods

Younger than springtime

A garden of a hat

Tall as a telegraph pole

Teeth like splinters

A dash of a dog

Eyes like drills

As smelly as a sock

USEFUL WORDS

as, comparison, like, lonely, of, smelly, smudge, splinters, springtime, teeth, telegraph, than, younger

1 Cover the pictures and read the comparisons. Describe the pictures you have in your mind. Use a chart like this:

Comparison	Picture
A smudge of a girl	a scruffy, grubby girl
As lonely as a cloud	

2 Draw the pictures which the following comparisons suggest:

a) a thatch of a hairstyle

b) fingers like sausages

c) as snug as a nest

d) ears like clothes-pegs

e) as still as a pond

f) a crate of a car.

a

1 List the words which are often used in comparisons.

2 Use these words to help you to write comparisons about:

a) an old gnarled tree

b) a bluetit busily pecking at nuts

c) a very light sponge cake

d) a contented cat

e) a sticky floor

f) curly hair.

b

Make notes of comparisons to use in a poem about one of the following:

◆ an old house

◆ a child in a bad temper

◆ a spider.

Write your poem and then read it aloud with a partner.

c

◆ Write your finished poem using a calligraphy felt-tipped pen.

◆ Draw pictures to illustrate the comparisons.

MAKE YOUR WORK LOOK GOOD!

47

Autumn

by Tony Langham

USEFUL WORDS

adjective, autumn, brown, calligram, crackle, decided, flicker, gold, hiss, leaf, leaves, orange, outline, russet, rustle, shape, slowly, smoke, spark, wisp, words

a

1 Read the poem aloud.
2 Write the words of the poem without the shape.
3 Read this new version aloud.
4 What difference does the shape make to the way in which you read the poem?

b

Write your own shape poem about autumn.

1 Find some other words about autumn.
2 Copy the shape of the poem.
3 Write your words on the leaves.

c

Make up a shape poem about a fire.

◆ List some adjectives and verbs about fire.
◆ Draw an outline of a fire with shapes large enough to write on.
◆ Write your poem on the shapes.

◆ Use 'fire colours' (oranges, reds, yellows) to colour your poem.
◆ Make a class display of everyone's poems.

MAKE YOUR WORK
LOOK GOOD!

24

Fast Food

You can make up performance poems about anything, including fast food!

USEFUL WORDS

anything, cheap, cheese, chorus, including, performance, poem, price, repeat, rhyme, rhythm, scene, shake, speech bubble, toast, verse

1 Read the poem aloud with your group.
2 Which lines make up the chorus?
3 How can you tell?
4 Write the pairs of rhyming words.

a

1 Make up two more lines for the poem. The rhyme bank will help.
2 Read them aloud to check the rhyme and rhythm.
3 Read the poem again with your group and take turns to add a pair of lines.

Rhyme bank

sauce	course
sausage roll	toad-in-the-hole
coffee	toffee
tea	agree, me
lemonade	paid
sausage and mash	corned beef hash
cherries	berries

b

Make up a performance poem about playtime.

◆ Before you begin, write some ideas for rhymes.
◆ Write a chorus.

c

◆ Draw the scene for your poem.
◆ Draw the speech bubbles very faintly.
◆ Write in the speech bubbles and cut them out.
◆ Glue them on to your picture.

MAKE YOUR WORK
LOOK GOOD!

25

The Witch

Alliteration is when words contain the same consonant sounds. This poem uses alliteration to create effects.

She comes by night, in fearsome flight,
in garments black as pitch,
the queen of doom upon her broom,
the wild and wicked witch,
a cackling crone with brittle bones   5
and desiccated limbs,
two evil eyes with warts and sties
and bags about the rims,
a dangling nose, ten twisted toes
and folds of shrivelled skin,   10
cracked and chipped and crackled lips
that frame a toothless grin.
She hurtles by, she sweeps the sky
and hurls a piercing screech.
As she swoops past, a spell is cast   15
on all her curses reach.
Take care to hide when the wild witch rides
to shriek her evil spell.
What she may do with a word or two
is much too grim to tell.   20

by Jack Prelutsky

USEFUL WORDS

alliteration, brittle, cackling, chipped, cracked, crackled, consonant, effect, fearsome, garments, hustle, line, piercing, pitch, screech, shrivelled, sound, verse, wicked, witch

1 Say the words 'fearsome flight' from the first line of the poem. Repeat them several times. What kind of effect do they create?

2 List other examples of alliteration from the poem. Underline the repeated consonant sounds. Make notes about their effects.

Example of alliteration	Effect created
wild and wicked witch	image of an evil witch charging around madly

a

1 Add another column to the chart above. In it write other words with the same sounds which add to the effect, for example: (*fearsome flight*) *forbidding, frightening, frightful*.

2 Write alliterative words to create the following effects:

Effect	A word to start you off	Alliterative words
sliding dangerously	slithering	
rushing about	dashing	
walking heavily and angrily	clomping	

Think of adjectives, nouns and verbs.

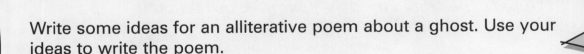

b

Write some ideas for an alliterative poem about a ghost. Use your ideas to write the poem.

c

◆ Write your poem in the shape of a ghost.
◆ Draw a ghostly background for it.

MAKE YOUR WORK LOOK GOOD!

26

Gunerania's Wedding Cake

These verses are from a poem written by a class of children.

The king he baked a wedding cake upon a
    sunny day,
The king he baked a wedding cake, it was in
    the month of May,
The king he baked a wedding cake, he filled it
    with old clocks,
A cabbage, and an octopus, some apples and
    red socks.
He mixed it, he whisked it, he threw it on
    the floor,   5
He crushed it, he mushed it, and it slithered
    out the door.

The king he baked a wedding cake and the glue he used was runny,
The king he baked a wedding cake with spiders and some honey,
The king he baked a wedding cake, he filled it with rusty nails,
A crocodile, a felt-tip pen, and a pinch of powdered snails.   10
He folded it, he moulded it, he squeezed it through his toes,
He sliced it, and diced it, 'til the flour went up his nose.

by Robert Soulsby and Class 1S, Brookvale Junior School

alternate, baked, cabbage, couplet, crushed, diced, end, folded, line,
mixed, moulded, mushed, pair, pattern, repeated, rhyme, rhyming,
rhythm, sliced, slithered, squeezed, verse, wedding, word

a

1 At which line of the poem do you realise that it is going to be funny?
2 Write the line you find the funniest.
3 Explain what makes it funny.

b

1 Which words in the poem are repeated?
2 Which of the following words describe the rhythm and rhyme pattern of the poem?

> *Write as many of the words as you need.*

| slow | quick | lively | gentle |

3 Write the words in the poem which rhyme with *day*, *clocks*, *mixed*, *crushed*, *floor*.
4 Which of the following rhyme patterns does the poem have?

> *There are two rhyme patterns in the poem.*

| the ends of alternate lines | the ends of pairs of lines which follow one another |

| the ends of every line | words in the same line |

c

Write another verse for the poem.

◆ List some useful rhyming words for your verse.
◆ Begin with the words *The king he baked a wedding cake ....*

◆ Write the poem on a piece of paper in the shape of a wedding cake.
◆ Each verse could be on a different layer of the cake.

> MAKE YOUR WORK LOOK GOOD!

27

Girls and Boys

This playscript is based on a passage from part of a story (Bill's New Frock by Anne Fine). One day, Bill Simpson woke up and was amazed to find that he was now a girl! The book tells about how people treated him differently from when he was a boy.

Scene: School hall
Cast: Headmaster

Bill Simpson ⎫
Astrid   ⎬ Pupils

Mrs Collins   Their teacher

The headmaster gazes around him. He picks four boys.

Astrid *(on the way out of the hall)*: It isn't fair, Mrs Collins! He *always* picks the boys to carry things.

Mrs Collins *(in a soothing voice)*: Perhaps the table's quite heavy.

Astrid: None of the tables in this school is heavy, and I know for a fact that I am stronger than at least two of the boys he picked.

Bill: It's true. Whenever we have a tug of war, everyone wants to have Astrid on their team.

Mrs Collins: Oh, well. It doesn't matter. No need to make such a fuss over nothing. It's only a silly old table.

Astrid and Bill take up arguing again.

Mrs Collins *(rather sharply)*: The subject is closed.

1 *Bill's New Frock* is written as prose, not as a playscript. Read the text below and compare it with the playscript.

a

> The headmaster gazed around him. Then he picked four boys.
> On the way out of the hall, Bill Simpson heard Astrid complaining to Mrs Collins:
> 'It isn't fair! He *always* picks the boys to carry things.'
> 'Perhaps the table's quite heavy,' soothed Mrs Collins.

2 Make notes about the differences between the playscript and prose. The chart will help.

	Playscript	Prose
Speech marks		
How it shows who is speaking		
How it shows how he or she speaks		
How it shows what the characters do		

b

1 Re-write the rest of the playscript as prose.
2 Read what you have written aloud with a partner. Does it sound right?

c

Choose a prose passage from a fiction book. Re-write it as a playscript.

Use the passage as a model.

◆ Glue your playscript on to a scroll.
◆ Roll it up and tie it with a ribbon. Open it when it is to be read.

MAKE YOUR WORK LOOK GOOD!

28

Skellig

Skellig *is about a boy called Michael who moves house and meets someone very unusual and special. This is the opening of chapter thirty. The writer creates the effect of the scene before writing about what happens.*

The owls woke me. Or a call that was like that of the owls. I looked out into the night. The moon hung over the city, a great orange ball with the silhouettes of steeples and chimney stacks upon it. The sky was blue around it, deepening to blackness high above, where only the most brilliant stars shone. Down below, the wilderness was filled with the pitch black shadow of the garage and a wedge of cold silvery light.

I watched for the birds and saw nothing.

'Skellig,' I whispered. 'Skellig. Skellig.'

USEFUL WORDS

adjective, atmosphere, brilliant, chimney, create, deepening, effect, exciting, light, mood, noun, pitch, scene, setting, silhouettes, silvery, special, unusual, watched, wedge, whispered, wilderness

1 Draw the scene described in the passage.

2 Which two of the adjectives below best describe the scene?

| bright | colourful | dark | noisy | quiet |

3 Write some words from the passage which create this effect.

4 Which adjective below best describes the atmosphere?

| cheerful | exciting | mysterious | sad | scary |

a

1 On a chart like this, list the adjectives in the passage:

Adjectives for colours	Adjectives about light or dark

2 Re-write the passage, changing the adjectives to create a different effect.

b

Write a description which sets the scene for an exciting story.

Use adjectives such as **bold, breathless, quick, silent, sudden**.

c

♦ Draw the scene you have described.

♦ Write the description in a border around the picture.

MAKE YOUR WORK LOOK GOOD!

The Worst Witch

This review is about the opening of the book, the characters, the main events and the ending.

The Worst Witch, written and illustrated by Jill Murphy, published by Puffin
This book is one of a series about a school for witches.

The opening describes the setting — Miss Cackle's Academy for Witches. At first it seems eerie, but you soon realise that the book is going to be about relationships in the school. The words which suggest this are 'There were so many rules that you couldn't do *anything* without being told off.'

The main character is Mildred, called 'the worst witch' because, however hard she tries, she gets things wrong. This makes you feel sorry for her. Her best friend, Maud, is likeable because she always supports Mildred. The headteacher, Miss Cackle, seems nice ('a pleasant grin'). Miss Hardbroom and Ethel seem nasty, although we see the nice side of Miss Hardbroom at the end of the story.

The main events of the story are the accidents and misfortunes which happen to Mildred. They lead up to a sad time when she runs away because she is upset about the trouble she is in, but saves the school from a group of witches who want to invade it. The school is given a holiday and Mildred is a heroine.

Everyone gets what he or she deserves, so it is a satisfying story.

USEFUL WORDS

although, author, characters, couldn't, describes, eerie, ending, headteacher, illustrator, main events, opening, publisher, pupils, relationships, review, setting, supports, teachers, witch, witches

1 What information does the review
   tell you about the author, illustrator and
   publisher?
2 What is the setting of the book?
3 Does the review make you want to read
   the book? Explain your answer.

a

What does the review tell you about the story? Write notes.
Copy and complete this chart:

Opening	Main character	Other characters	Main events	Ending

b

Write a review of a book you have read.

◆ Begin by writing the title and the name of
   the author, illustrator and publisher.
◆ Write about the setting, the characters,
   the opening, the main events and the
   ending.

c

◆ Use the headings in the chart above to organise
   your review.
◆ Draw a picture of the cover of the book. Include
   the title, the author's name and anything else you
   see on it.

MAKE YOUR WORK
LOOK GOOD!

This is an extract from the Toytown telephone directory.
People are listed alphabetically by their family names.

Peep, Bo 5 Sheep Lane, Toytown TO3 6NY **01234 009987**

Shafto, Bobby Harbour House, The Quayside, Toytown TO9 9PL **01234 886644**

Sprat, Jack 5 Meat Street, Toytown TO1 3GF **01234 224530**

Tucker, Tommy 40 Supper Lane, Toytown TO9 7PK **01234 67546**

White, Snow Dwarf Cottage, Bashful Street, Toytown TO8 7DD **01234 564783**

Wincey, Incey 8 Spider Way, Toytown TO3 5SP **01234 541809**

Contrary, Mary Garden House, Pretty Maid Street, Toytown TO8 8KL **01234 670695**

Dumpty, Humpty The Wall, Wall Street, Toytown TO6 2NN **01234 989800**

Foster, Dr G. Gloucester Place, Toytown TO7 9GG **01234 873241**

Goose, Mother 8 Egg Avenue, Toytown TO9 7YG **01234 893421**

Horner, Jack Plum Corner, Thumb Road, Toytown TO1 0QW **01234 087712**

Locket, Lucy Pocket House, Toytown TO9 0PL **01234 351093**

USEFUL WORDS

address, alphabet, alphabetical, alphabetically, chart, column, directory, family, list, name, order, people, personal, row, telephone

62

1 Why are telephone directories arranged alphabetically?

2 Write the characters' names in the way in which they appear in the stories or rhymes.

3 Jack Sprat and Bobby Shafto both begin with 's'. Why is Bobby Shafto listed first?

4 Snow White and Incey Wincey both begin with 'w'. Why is Snow White listed first?

a

1 Write the personal names and family names of the people in your group.

2 Write their names in the way in which they would appear in a telephone directory.

3 Write their addresses and telephone numbers.

4 Arrange the directory entries in alphabetical order.

b

Key the names and addresses of your group into a word-processed chart.

♦ Use the computer to sort them alphabetically.

c

♦ Make parts of your chart **bold** to help the reader find people's names.

♦ Decide if you want to print the lines between the columns and rows on the chart.

MAKE YOUR WORK LOOK GOOD!

Acknowledgements

The publishers gratefully acknowledge copyright holders for permission to use copyright material. Every effort has been made to trace copyright holders and to obtain their permission for the use of copyright material. The author and publishers will gladly receive information enabling them to rectify any error or omission in subsequent editions.

Unit 2: text: from *Soccer Shadows* by Rob Childs (Corgi, 2002), reprinted by permission of Transworld Publishers, a division of The Random House Group Ltd; **Unit 3**: text: from *No Problem, Davy* by Peggy Burns (Lion Publishing, 1991), copyright © Peggy Burns 1991, reprinted by permission of the publishers; **Unit 5**: text: from *The Hundred-Mile-an-Hour Dog* by Jeremy Strong (Penguin Puffin, 1996), reprinted by permission of David Higham Associates; **Unit 9**: text: from the Bible (Matthew 13:1–9, Mark 4:1–9, Luke 8:4–8); **Unit 10**: text: adapted from *The Little Match Girl* by Hans Christian Andersen; **Unit 11**: text: from *Mr Majeika on the Internet* by Humphrey Carpenter (Penguin Puffin, 2001), copyright © Humphrey Carpenter 2001, reprinted by permission of Penguin Books Ltd; **Unit 12**: text: from *George's Marvellous Medicine* by Roald Dahl (Jonathan Cape, 1981; Penguin Puffin, 1982), copyright © Roald Dahl 1981, reprinted by permission of David Higham Associates; **Unit 23**: poem: 'Autumn' by Tony Langham, copyright © Tony Langham 1998, first published in John Foster (ed.): *Word Whirls, and Other Shape Poems* (OUP, 1998), reprinted by permission of the author; **Unit 25**: poem: 'The Witch' by Jack Prelutsky, from *Nightmares: Poems to Trouble Your Sleep* (A&C Black, 1976), copyright © Jack Prelutsky 1976, reprinted by permission of the publishers; **Unit 26**: lines from poem: 'Gunerania's Wedding Cake' by Robert Soulsby and Class lS, Brookvale Junior School, first published in Michael Rosen (ed.): *Pilly Soems: Michael Rosen's Book of Very Silly Poems* (A&C Black, 1994) reprinted by permission of Robert Soulsby; **Unit 27**: text: from *Bill's New Frock* by Anne Fine (Mammoth, 1989), copyright © Anne Fine 1989, reprinted by permission of the publisher, Egmont Books Ltd, London; adaptation by permission of David Higham Associates; **Unit 28**: text: from *Skellig* by David Almond (Hodder, 1998), reprinted by permission of Hodder & Stoughton Ltd.

Illustrations

Linda Jeffrey, Units 1, 4, 8, 11, 17, 22, 25, 27, 29
Carol Jonas, Units 3, 5, 10, 13, 15, 21, 23 (p.49), 26, 30
Ruth Palmer, Units 2, 6, 7, 9, 12, 14, 16, 20, 24, 28